PAUSE

The Power of Intentional Rest

DR. STACIA THOMPSON

Dedication

To my incredible son, my greatest teacher, who showed me the profound beauty of presence and the absolute necessity of slowing down. Your boundless joy and the way you simply *are* in the world remind me daily that the most precious moments aren't found in the hustle, but in the quiet, intentional pauses. You are my heart's rhythm and my ultimate "why."

To my phenomenal village—my family and friends. You are the steadfast anchors in my life, the ones who held me up when I felt like I was crumbling, who listened without judgment, and who constantly reminded me that it's more than okay to receive. Your love, your unwavering belief, and your willingness to show up for me have been the very foundation of this entire journey. You truly embody the peace and connection I write about.

And to my ancestors, whose wildest dreams might just have been the very rest and peace we now strive to reclaim.

Thank you for your resilience, your sacrifices, and for paving the way. I carry your strength and honor your journey by choosing a path of well-being.

Finally, to every single soul who has ever felt the relentless pressure to "do more," "be more," and "hustle harder"— this book is for you. May you find within these pages the permission, the practical tools, and the fierce courage to reclaim your peace, honor your unique rhythm, and live a life that is truly rested, deeply aligned, and overflowing with joy. You are inherently worthy of the pause.

CONTENTS

PAUSE

THE POWER OF INTENTIONAL REST

Introduction

Welcome, dear reader, to your journey of intentional rest and mindfulness. This book is your companion on the journey to embrace the power of the pause, redefine success on your own terms, and cultivate a life overflowing with peace and purpose. Just as my story unfolds within these pages—a candid reflection of my path from relentless "rise and grind" to intentional rest—this book invites you to explore your own rhythm. Here, you'll find space to listen to your body's whispers, challenge old beliefs about productivity, and design a life where rest isn't a luxury, but your most powerful tool for well-being. Pause ≠ Stop. Let's be clear, pausing doesn't mean quitting. It doesn't mean abandoning your ambition, ignoring your responsibilities, or letting everything go. To pause means to break the loop, to breathe, to recalibrate. It is an active, intentional act of checking in. Pausing says: I care enough to slow down and listen before I move forward again. Grab your favorite beverage, find a comfortable space, and let's begin your unique pause journey.

CHAPTER 1

Embracing the Pause

Origin story, burnout, redefining success

The First Pause

It's kind of ironic, right? I'm writing a book about how important it is to pause, but the world we live in is all about going, going, going. We're always told that being busy means you're valuable and being productive is the same as having a purpose. But what if, while we're chasing all that "more," we're missing out on what makes life meaningful? What if the real key to a better, more effective life is to stop and pause—on purpose?

For me, this wasn't some lightbulb moment. It was a gradual thing, and sometimes, yeah, it was painful. It started with this feeling that something was just...off.

I remember when I landed my first leadership role and was determined to prove myself. I was working nonstop, running on pure ambition and, let's be honest, a fear of messing up. I was always on the move—traveling for work, in meetings, dealing with a million to-dos. Work and life? They just blurred into one big, crazy mess.

And on the outside, it looked like I was killing it. I was hitting my goals, getting recognized, and moving up the ladder. But inside, I was a mess. I was exhausted, stressed out, and totally disconnected from what really mattered: family, friends, and me. And the travel, which should have been fun, felt like another thing on my to-do list. I was so focused on getting there that I forgot to enjoy the ride. I could feel myself hitting a wall. The pressure was building and I knew I couldn't keep going like that. It wasn't just being tired; it was this deep, bone-tired exhaustion that no sleep could fix. I was losing my joy, my passion, my sense of who I was.

Then, one day, it all kind of crashed. It was a normal day. I dropped my son off at school and instead of rushing to the office, I just felt this huge urge to...stop. To pause. I didn't call in "sick" in the usual way. I didn't have a fever or anything. But I was sick. I was sick of the constant pressure, the always-hustling, and this feeling that I was missing my own life.

That day, I made a choice. I decided to take a day for myself. A mental health day. This wasn't a vacation day. It wasn't a day to catch up on errands or chores. It was a day to do absolutely nothing. I didn't open my laptop. I didn't check my email. I didn't answer work calls. I just let myself be.

I remember feeling guilty at first. That little voice in my head said, "You should be working. You're being lazy. You're letting everyone down." But I pushed those thoughts away. I knew, deep down, that I needed this.

That first mental health day changed everything. I spent the day doing simple things: reading, listening to music, and taking a long bath. I even let myself veg out and watch mindless TV and eat. It was a day of pure rest and relaxation. And something amazing happened.

When I allowed myself to slow down, to disconnect from all the noise and demands, I started to reconnect with myself. I started to hear my own voice again, the voice that had been drowned out by the constant chaos of my busy life. I remembered what brought me joy, what made me feel alive, and what was truly important.

That day was a turning point. It was the first pause, the moment I made a conscious choice to put my well-being first. It was the start of a journey—a journey that's taught me how incredibly powerful it is to pause. It wasn't just about taking a day off now and then. It was about changing my whole perspective and seeing that rest and self-care aren't luxuries—they're necessities. It was about realizing I'm not a machine and my worth isn't about how much I produce.

I've been lucky to have people who reinforced this along the way. I remember a VP I worked for who always said we're "no good to others if we are no good to ourselves." That stuck with me. It was a reminder that taking care of myself wasn't selfish; it was essential, not just for me, but for how I lead and help others.

Naming the Gap: From Hustle to Harmony

You know, it's funny... success used to be something very external to me. It was all about the achievements, the titles, the recognition, the constant forward motion. It was about proving myself, climbing the ladder, and keeping up with this crazy fast pace. I used to measure my worth by my productivity, by how much I could get done in a day, a week, a year. Rest? Rest was almost an enemy. It felt like I was losing time, falling behind. There was this constant pressure to be "on," to be available, to be producing. If I wasn't actively doing something, I felt like I wasn't being valuable.

This gap between that old definition and where I am now is huge. It's like night and day. Now, success is so much more about internal things. It's about well-being, peace, and fulfillment. Don't get me wrong, I still have goals and I'm driven to make a difference. But I've learned that true success isn't sustainable without incorporating rest and it's not just about the big achievements. It's also about the small everyday moments. It's about the quality of my relationships, my health, and my mental and emotional state.

Rest is fundamental to this new definition. It's not an afterthought; it's a core component. I see it now as the foundation that everything else is built on. It's the fuel that allows me to be productive, creative, and effective in the long run. When I'm rested, I'm more focused, resilient, and able to handle challenges. But beyond that, rest is essential for my overall well-being. It allows me to be present, to enjoy life, and to connect with myself and others on a deeper level. The gap between the two is like the difference between constantly running on fumes and driving a fully charged electric car. Both will get you somewhere, but one is far more sustainable, efficient, and enjoyable.

Lessons from the Jamaica Scare

That trip to Jamaica...that was a major wake-up call. It happened about a year into a new role and I was going non-stop. Day and night, around the clock, attending community events, late nights, early mornings —I was afraid of missing anything. I felt like I had to be at every single event. I arrived in Jamaica on a Friday, and by Sunday, I was in a Jamaican hospital. I thought it was just a bad headache or maybe my sinuses, that I could sleep it off.

Hindsight being 20/20, I learned a couple of crucial lessons and I've also picked up a couple of things I'll always do going forward: get travel insurance (thankfully, I did!) and wear a smartwatch. That smartwatch? It probably saved my life. While I was trying to rest in my room, the watch kept alerting me that my resting heart rate was 120. I was on this group trip and two of our friends were nurses. I messaged them about what my watch said and they immediately came to my room. They took one look at me, and while one went to get a wheelchair, the other put my sunglasses on me and wrapped me in a blanket to take me to the infirmary. They determined my blood pressure was dangerously high and I was severely dehydrated. They sent me straight to the emergency room. And $931 later…I didn't want them to run more tests, so I spent the rest of the trip in bed. As soon as I got home, I went to my own ER, where they told me I had pneumonia! I was sure glad that travel insurance covered that ER visit in Jamaica. I was also really glad that I followed that old wives' tale about leaving for vacation with a clean house, because I was in no condition to do anything but rest when I got back.

That whole experience really hit me hard. It showed me that I have to recognize I'm only one person and I have to remember that. It's not necessary to try to attend every thing I'm invited to in my professional and personal life. I was trying to do it all and my body just completely shut down. **What should have been a pause—a time for relaxation and enjoyment—became an expensive bed rest, costing me time, money, and my health. It was a stark awakening that forced me to reevaluate how to balance my time, where and how I show up, and how to truly prioritize my well-being.**

This is your invitation to pause. Let's step into it, together.

Reflection Prompts for Chapter 1: Embracing the Pause

- What did your body know before your mind was willing to admit it? Describe the physical sensations, emotional states, or recurring thoughts trying to alert you to your need for rest.

- Can you identify a specific breaking point or turning point where exhaustion became clear? What circumstances surrounded this moment? What insights emerged?

- How did you feel—emotionally and physically— during this breaking point? What emotions surfaced as you finally acknowledged your need to pause?

- How has your definition of success shifted in the last five years? What does "success" mean to you now, beyond external achievements?

- Write a letter to your former self who still believes rest is laziness or a luxury you couldn't afford. What wisdom would you share? What reassurance does this former self need to hear? What permission do they need to receive?

CHAPTER 2

Mindful Moments

---

*Present awareness, body cues,
emotional stillness*

Body Wisdom: Listening to Your Body's Whispers

I think we've all had those moments where our body tries to tell us something, but we're too busy or too focused to listen. We ignore the little signs, the whispers, until they become screams. I have a vivid memory of a time when my body was practically shouting at me to slow down, but my mind was too preoccupied to hear it. It was about a month before my dissertation defense, a time when stress levels were through the roof.

I was at a routine doctor's appointment and the nurse took my blood pressure. "Elevated," she said. We waited, took it again. Still high. She asked if I had any stress in my life. I just laughed and said, "My whole life." LOL. She wrote it off as stress or "white coat syndrome." She asked if I was tired. I told her I was always tired, but that I'd been dealing with insomnia. Her suggestion? "If you start feeling more tired or have other symptoms, go to prompt care."

A few days later, I wasn't feeling well. I had flu-like symptoms and something was just...off. I was heading into work and decided to stop at the prompt care on the way. By chance, I knew the nurse who called me back. She took my blood pressure and asked if it had ever been elevated, or if I had high blood pressure. I told her no. We waited, took it again. She shook her head, left the room, and called my primary care physician because of how high it was. I ended up on bed rest for the weekend. My mom stopped by to check on me. I must have looked like death warmed over because she took one look at me and told me to stay in bed and not even think about going to church on Sunday!

Looking back, it's clear my body was sending out distress signals long before I finally crashed. The insomnia, the constant tiredness, even the elevated blood pressure at that first appointment—those were all whispers. I ignored them, attributing them to stress and a demanding schedule.

I was going so hard—work, dissertation defense prep, extracurriculars, everything—with no rest. My body was telling me to sit down and take several seats. This doctor's visit was a profound moment for me. It was my body unequivocally telling me the truth I didn't want to hear. This moment forced me to truly listen, realizing how differently things could have ended had I not sought medical attention. It was also the first time I genuinely believed the statement that stress can literally kill you.

Stop Asking Your Body for Forgiveness Instead of Permission

This phrase hits home for me because for years, I lived it. I'd push myself to the absolute brink, ignoring every whisper, every ache, every sign of exhaustion. My body would scream for a break, but I'd silence it, telling myself I'd "make up for it later." I'd work through lunch, skip workouts, sacrifice sleep, and then, only when I was completely depleted, would I finally collapse, asking my body for "forgiveness" for the abuse I'd put it through.

This reactive approach is incredibly damaging. It turns our bodies into battlegrounds, where we constantly fight against our natural needs, only to surrender when we have no other choice. The shift, the true "pause" moment, comes when we flip that script. Instead of waiting for a breakdown to grant ourselves permission to rest, we ask for permission before the damage is done.

This means proactively listening to the subtle cues: the first yawn, the slight tension in the shoulders, the fleeting thought of "I need a break." It means honoring those signals as valid requests, not inconveniences. It's about building trust with our bodies—where we respect their limits and anticipate their needs—rather than relentlessly pushing them past their breaking point.

This proactive permission-giving is a radical act of self-care. It's about recognizing that our bodies aren't machines designed for endless output; they are intricate, sensitive systems that require consistent nourishment and rest. When we give ourselves permission to pause, we're not just preventing burnout; we're cultivating a deeper respect for our own well-being, fostering resilience, and ultimately, creating a more sustainable and joyful life. It's about moving from a mindset of depletion to one of proactive preservation.

The Gift of Rest

That time my mentor gave me her vacation days... that was a huge lesson for me. It wasn't just about the time off; it was about something much deeper. You see, I've always been the person who gets things done. If someone wasn't pulling their weight, or things weren't moving quickly enough, I'd jump in and say, "I'll help," or, "I'll just do it myself." I took pride in being self-sufficient, in being the one people could rely on. So, when my mentor offered me her vacation days, it forced me to confront something I hadn't really dealt with before: my difficulty in receiving help.

It was uncomfortable, to say the least. I had to learn to... accept. Accept that it was okay to need support, that it was okay to not be the one always giving it. It taught me that asking for help, and accepting it when offered, isn't a sign of weakness. It's not a character flaw. It's actually a sign of strength, of self-awareness. It takes courage to be vulnerable, to admit you can't do it all on your own.

I learned that there's no shame in needing support. We've all heard the saying, "It takes a village to raise a child." Well, I've learned that, hell, it takes a village to help me. And that's okay. It's about recognizing that we're all interconnected, that we all need each other sometimes. It's about building a community of support, where we can both give and receive without hesitation.

Listening for God's Whisper

In the moments of quiet, that's when I can really take time to refocus. Life gets so noisy, you know? Between work, family, and just trying to keep up with everything, it's easy to get completely lost in the chaos. But it's when things get still, when all that external noise fades away, that I can truly hear that still, small voice. For me, that's God's voice, and it's in those quiet moments that I find my clarity, my direction. It's when I can reflect, pray, and listen to what my soul is trying to tell me. I have my best thoughts and reflections in the shower while listening to praise and worship music. That's actually where I come up with my best ideas, too.

It's in these moments of stillness that I find myself reconnecting with my purpose, my pace, and my worth. When I silence the noise of the world, I can hear the gentle whisper of God guiding me. This could be during my morning meditation, a quiet walk in nature, or simply sitting in contemplation. It's during these times that I'm reminded of who I am, what I'm here to do, and that I am valued and loved unconditionally. The silence also helps me discern whether I'm on the right path and I'm moving at a sustainable pace. Am I pushing myself too hard? Am I taking on too much? Or am I moving in alignment with my values and my calling? It's in the silence that I find the courage to say "no" to things that drain me and "yes" to things that give me life. For me, silence has clarified my calling. It has helped me to understand that my work in the world is not just about achieving goals or acquiring accolades, but about serving others, making a difference, and leaving a positive impact.

This concept of intentional pausing, whether a full mental health day or a small ritual, reminds me of the biblical term "Selah." You see it sprinkled throughout the Psalms, and it's often interpreted as a pause, a moment to reflect, to uplift, to truly consider what's just been said or experienced. It's not just a break in the music; it's an invitation to let the words sink in, to absorb the meaning, to allow your spirit to catch up with your mind. These mental health days, these moments of "me time," are my personal Selah. They're where I intentionally hit pause on the relentless rhythm of life, allowing myself to truly process, breathe, and reconnect with my inner peace and my Creator. It's in these sacred pauses that true rejuvenation happens, allowing me to return to the world not just rested, but deeply refreshed and ready to face whatever comes next.

Learning to Be Still

In those moments when I've allowed myself to truly stop, breathe, and be still, I've discovered some important things about myself. I've realized that at times I set the bar too high and create unrealistic expectations and promises. When I'm constantly on the go, I tend to overcommit and take on more than I can realistically handle. This can lead to feelings of overwhelm, stress, and disappointment when I inevitably fall short of my own expectations.

I've also recognized things that need to be prioritized at home often get pushed to the back burner. When I'm so focused on external commitments, household tasks and chores can pile up, leading to clutter and disarray. This, in turn, can cause anxiety, as a disorganized environment can negatively impact my stress levels. It's distracting and can contribute to an overall feeling of chaos.

Learning to be still has helped me to become more aware of these patterns and their impact on my well-being. It has allowed me to reassess my priorities, taking a step back to evaluate what truly matters to me, both personally and professionally. This helps me make more conscious choices about how I spend my time and energy. By understanding my limits and capabilities, I can set goals that are achievable and sustainable, reducing the pressure to constantly overachieve and preventing burnout. I've also learned to establish healthy boundaries, saying "no" to commitments that don't align with my priorities or that would compromise my well-being, which helps me to protect my time and energy and create more space for rest and self-care. I strive to create a more balanced life by integrating all aspects of myself, including work, relationships, hobbies, and rest, allowing me to feel more fulfilled and less stressed. Finally, stillness allows me to slow down and savor the simple things in life, cultivating gratitude and a sense of peace.

The Importance of Sleep

"I only need a couple of hours of sleep" is the biggest lie ever told. This statement resonates deeply because, for too long, I, like many, wore a lack of sleep as a badge of honor, a sign of my dedication and hustle. "I'll sleep when I'm dead," was a common, albeit dangerous, mantra. But I've learned, often the hard way, that neglecting sleep isn't just about feeling tired; it's a direct assault on our physical, mental, and emotional health. The idea that we can thrive on minimal sleep is a pervasive myth, that actively undermines our well-being and long-term sustainability. Simply put, sleep deprivation occurs when you consistently get less sleep than your body needs. For most adults, that sweet spot is typically 7-9 hours per night. It's not just about pulling an all-nighter once in a while; it's the cumulative effect of chronic insufficient sleep that truly does the damage. It's living in a constant state of "sleep debt," where your body and mind are perpetually playing catch-up, and never quite getting there.

What happens when you don't get enough sleep? The unhealthy effects: The consequences of chronic sleep deprivation are far-reaching and, frankly, terrifying. It's not just about feeling groggy; it impacts every system in our body and every aspect of our lives. We must get proper rest because it's foundational to our very existence. Here are just some of the unhealthy effects and the serious diseases and disorders it can cause:

- **Cognitive Impairment:** This is one I felt acutely. Lack of sleep severely impacts our ability to concentrate, focus, remember information, and make sound decisions. Our reaction time slows and our judgment becomes impaired. It's like trying to think through a fog. You might find yourself making more mistakes, struggling to learn new things, or having difficulty with problem-solving.

- **Mood Disturbances:** Irritability, mood swings, increased stress, anxiety, and even symptoms of depression become much more prevalent. Our emotional regulation goes right out the window. Little things can set you off and you might feel a persistent sense of unease or sadness.

- **Weakened Immune System:** When we don't get enough sleep, our bodies produce fewer infection-fighting antibodies and protective cytokines. This leaves us more vulnerable to common illnesses like colds and flu and can prolong recovery times. My pneumonia scare in Jamaica was a direct result of this—my body simply couldn't fight off infection because it was too depleted.

- **Increased Risk of Accidents:** Impaired reaction time and reduced alertness significantly increase the risk of car accidents, workplace incidents, and other mishaps. Drowsy driving is as dangerous as drunk driving and studies show that being awake for 18 hours can impair your driving as much as a blood alcohol content of 0.05%.

- **Weight Gain and Obesity:** Sleep deprivation disrupts hormones that regulate appetite (ghrelin, which increases hunger, and leptin, which signals fullness). This leads to increased hunger, cravings for high-calorie, high-carbohydrate foods, and a slower metabolism. It's a vicious cycle that makes weight management incredibly difficult.

- **Cardiovascular Disease:** Chronic lack of sleep has been linked to an increased risk of high blood pressure, heart disease, stroke, and diabetes. Our heart works harder when it doesn't get sufficient rest and inflammation markers increase.

- **Diabetes:** Sleep deprivation can affect how our bodies process glucose, increasing insulin resistance and raising the risk of developing Type 2 diabetes. Even a few nights of insufficient sleep can make healthy individuals show signs of pre-diabetes.

- **Hormonal Imbalances:** Beyond appetite hormones, sleep impacts growth hormone (crucial for repair), stress hormones (cortisol levels remain elevated), and even reproductive hormones, leading to a cascade of potential issues throughout the body.

- **Mental Health Disorders:** While not always a direct cause, chronic sleep deprivation is a significant risk factor for developing or worsening mental health conditions like anxiety disorders, depression, and even psychosis in vulnerable individuals. It creates a fertile ground for these issues to take root and flourish.

- **Reduced Physical Performance:** Our strength, endurance, and coordination all suffer when we're sleep-deprived. Recovery from exercise is also compromised, making it harder for muscles to repair and grow. Athletes, in particular, know that sleep is a crucial part of their training regimen.

In summary, prioritizing quality sleep isn't a luxury; it's a fundamental pillar of mindful living and overall well-being. Proper rest isn't a luxury; it's a biological imperative. It's during sleep that our bodies repair themselves, our brains consolidate memories, process emotions, and clear out metabolic waste. It's when our immune system recharges and our hormones rebalance. To deny ourselves this fundamental need is to actively undermine our health, happiness, and ability to live a full, vibrant life. We must prioritize sleep not just to survive, but to thrive truly. Give yourself permission to go to sleep early. There's a sacred rhythm in winding down early. I call it a single-digit bedtime, when you intentionally go to bed before 10 p.m. Not because you're exhausted, but because you're prioritizing recovery.

Sleep is one of the most underrated acts of resistance in a hustle culture. Getting into bed while others are still "grinding" is a bold declaration: I choose my wellness.

Try it once a week. No screens. No guilt. Just rest.

Resting Can Be Hard Because:

- **You associate rest with laziness.** For so long, I believed that if I wasn't actively producing, I was falling behind—a sentiment deeply ingrained by hustle culture. Unlearning this takes conscious effort and a redefinition of what 'valuable' truly means. It's a societal narrative that tells us our worth is tied to our output, making rest feel like a moral failing rather than a biological necessity.

- **You were taught to do everything on your own.** Many of us grew up in environments where self-sufficiency was highly praised, sometimes to the exclusion of interdependence. This can make it incredibly difficult to ask for or accept help, even when we're drowning. The idea of delegating or relying on others for support can feel like a sign of weakness, rather than a smart strategy for managing capacity.

- **You struggle with asking for help.** This ties into the previous point. The act of reaching out and admitting you can't do it all can feel vulnerable. Yet, true strength often lies in recognizing your limits and building a supportive community around you. It's a muscle that needs to be exercised, and the more you practice, the easier it becomes.

- **You feel guilty for prioritizing your needs.** This is a common internal battle, especially for parents and caregivers. The "shoulds" creep in: "I should be working," "I should be doing more for my family," "I should be helping my friends." This guilt can be a powerful saboteur, making you feel unworthy of rest even when your body and mind desperately crave it. As parents and caregivers, the guilt of taking time for ourselves can be immense, but remember: you cannot pour from an empty cup. Prioritizing your well-being is not selfish; it is essential for you to show up fully and effectively for those who rely on you. Learning to silence this guilt is a crucial step in embracing the pause.

- **You don't trust others to help.** When you're used to doing everything yourself, it's hard to let go. There's a fear that if you don't do it, it won't get done right—or won't get done at all. This lack of trust can burden you with unnecessary tasks and prevent you from truly delegating or stepping back. Building trust in others and in your ability to guide them is essential.

- **You're the default parent.** For many, especially mothers, the role of "default parent" means constant availability and responsibility for everything from school schedules to emotional support. This can make finding personal time feel impossible, as every moment seems to be claimed by the needs of your children. It requires intentional boundary setting and seeking support from partners or your wider community.

- **You measure your worth based on your productivity.** This is a deeply ingrained belief in a society that glorifies busyness. When your self-worth is tied to how much you accomplish rest feels like a threat to your identity. Redefining success on your own terms, as we discussed in Chapter 1, is vital to breaking free from this cycle. Your inherent worth is not dependent on your output.

- **You lack boundaries.** Without clear boundaries, your time and energy become an open invitation for others' demands. This can lead to a constant feeling of being stretched thin and overwhelmed. Learning to say "no" with grace, to protect your schedule, and to communicate your limits is fundamental to creating space for rest.

- **You believe rest is a sign of weakness or failure.** This harmful belief is a direct offshoot of hustle culture. It suggests that strong, successful people never stop, never rest. In reality, consistent rest is a sign of strength, resilience, and smart self-management. It's a proactive strategy for long-term success, not a weakness.

- **You don't know how.** Sometimes, the biggest barrier is simply not knowing where to start. If you've been running on empty for years, the very idea of rest can feel foreign or overwhelming. This book is designed to provide the practical tools and mindset shifts to overcome this, guiding you step-by-step into a more rested life.

Reflection Prompts for Chapter 2: Mindful Moments

- What does your body whisper to you when you're still? What sensations, emotions, or thoughts arise when you allow yourself to just be?

- Describe a moment where silence or stillness brought you a breakthrough, a new insight, or a profound sense of peace.

- How do you experience God or your spiritual side differently in stillness than in motion?

- What are your "tells"—those physical, emotional, or mental signs that you're carrying too much and need to pause?

- What would it look like to consciously plan stillness into your week? Be specific about when and how you might do this.

CHAPTER 3

Creating Your Pause Plan

---

*Boundaries, lifestyle shift,
sustainable rhythm*

Defining Success on Your Terms

My relationship with rest has definitely been a journey, evolving as I've grown, not only in my career—from support staff to leader, from uncertain coach to confident mentor—but also in my understanding of myself. In the past, especially in those early support staff roles, rest was often an afterthought, something I'd grab if I had time, rather than something I actively prioritized. It was very much a "get the work done" mentality.

As I transitioned into leadership and coaching, the demands shifted and I began to see the connection between my well-being and my ability to effectively guide and support others. Initially, as I stepped into the coaching space, there was a period of uncertainty. I was pouring a lot of energy into learning and establishing myself and rest was still somewhat on the back burner. However, as I gained confidence and experience, particularly in mentoring others, I recognized that I couldn't sustain that pace without burning out. More importantly, I realized that I wasn't modeling a healthy approach to work and life for those I was guiding. I had to show them how to effectively guide and support others, which meant taking care of myself too. Now, I can recognize the need for rest and plan for it before I hit my wall. I can feel myself approaching that wall, and I know when to pull back. I have to live as an example since I encourage others to do it as well.

I'm very intentional about my pause. I understand that rest isn't just physical; it's also mental and physiological. It's about taking the time to recharge in all those areas. And I'm open about that with those I encounter and in my circle of influence. I talk about it, I schedule it, and I protect it. We lead by example. As a leader and a mentor, I've come to see that one of the most important things I can model is a healthy relationship with rest. It's about demonstrating that it's okay—and necessary—to prioritize well-being, set boundaries, and disconnect in order to recharge. This shift has not only made me more effective and sustainable in my roles, but it has also fundamentally changed how I define success. Success is no longer just about external achievements; it's about creating a life that is both fulfilling and sustainable, a life where rest is an integral part of the equation.

Breaking the Cycle

For so long, I was caught in a cycle—a self-made loop of overcommitment, relentless striving, and the subtle, nagging belief that I always had to be doing something. Breaking this cycle wasn't easy because it meant challenging deeply ingrained habits and external pressures. It meant saying "no" when every fiber of my being wanted to say "yes" just to please or to avoid missing out. It meant learning to delegate, even when I worried it wouldn't be done "my way." It meant letting go of the need to control every outcome and trusting that things would still get done, even if I wasn't the one doing them. This breaking of the cycle is an ongoing practice, a constant recalibration, but it's essential for creating genuine space for the pause. It's about choosing freedom over perceived obligation and knowing that my capacity is finite, but my spirit is boundless when nurtured.

Time: Your Irreplaceable Currency

I told my students that you can always make more money, but time is something you can never get back. This isn't just a catchy phrase; it's a fundamental truth that underpins the entire philosophy of the pause. In our society, we're conditioned to chase financial gain, to believe that more money equates to more security, more happiness, more freedom. And while financial stability is certainly important, it's crucial to recognize the profound difference between a renewable resource like money and afinite one like time.

You can earn back money you've lost. You can find new sources of income, invest, save, or even win the lottery. But every single second that ticks by is gone forever. You can't earn back a missed moment with a loved one, a sunset you didn't see because you were too busy, or a period of rest you sacrificed for an arbitrary deadline. This realization shifts the entire paradigm of how we value our lives and well-being.

When we prioritize our time, we are, in essence, prioritizing our lives. We are choosing to invest in experiences, relationships, health, and peace, knowing that these are the true currencies of a rich and fulfilling existence. It means consciously deciding that an extra hour of sleep, a quiet moment of reflection, or an afternoon spent pursuing a joyful hobby is infinitely more valuable than pushing ourselves to the brink for an extra dollar or a perceived professional advantage.

This isn't about being irresponsible with finances; it's about being profoundly responsible with your life. It's about recognizing that the pursuit of "more" can often lead to the loss of what truly matters. When you understand that time is your most precious and irreplaceable asset, you begin to guard it fiercely, setting boundaries with grace, saying "no" with conviction, and intentionally carving out moments for what truly nourishes your soul. This is the ultimate investment, one that pays dividends in peace, joy, and a life lived fully present.

The Power of Affirmations: Speaking Your Pause into Being

If you say you're going to "try" to change your schedule, or "try" to take a break, "try" to get more rest, that leaves it open-ended. It creates an escape hatch, a subtle permission to fall back into old patterns when things get tough. The language we use, both internally and externally, holds immense power. It shapes our beliefs, influences our actions, and determines our reality. Instead of saying and believing "I am going to *try* to get rest," or "I am going to *try* to take a break," or "I am going to *try* to change my schedule," we need to shift to definitive, affirmative language: "I *am* going to get rest," "I *am* taking a break," "I *am* changing my schedule."

This isn't just semantics; it's a fundamental shift in mindset. When you use "try," you're acknowledging a possibility of failure, keeping one foot out the door. When you use "I am," you're making a declaration, a commitment to yourself. You're activating your internal resolve and setting a clear intention for your brain and body to follow. This is the essence of an affirmation: a positive statement that, when repeated and believed, can help you challenge and overcome self-sabotaging thoughts.

Why Affirmations Work for Your Pause Plan:

- **Reprogramming Your Subconscious:** Our brains are wired for what we tell them repeatedly. If you constantly say "I'm so busy," your brain will find ways to keep you busy. If you affirm, "I prioritize my peace and rest," your subconscious mind starts looking for opportunities to make that true. This isn't magic; it's neuroscience. The reticular activating system (RAS) in your brain acts like a filter, highlighting what you focus on. By affirming your intentions, you train your RAS to notice opportunities for rest and peace.

- **Building Self-Efficacy:** When you speak with certainty, you build confidence in your ability to achieve your goals. This self-efficacy is crucial when trying to break old, ingrained habits of overwork. Each time you declare "I am taking a break" and then follow through, you reinforce your belief in your agency and ability to create change.

- **Creating a New Narrative:** You're actively rewriting the "hustle narrative" within your mind. Each affirmation is a brick in the foundation of your new, sustainable rhythm. You're replacing limiting beliefs ("I must always be productive") with empowering truths ("My worth is inherent, not earned through endless doing").

- **Holding Yourself Accountable:** Affirmations aren't just whispers; they can be powerful public declarations to yourself. When you say, "I am taking a mental health day," you're less likely to let external pressures derail you because you've already committed to it internally. It creates a sense of integrity with yourself.

How to Integrate Affirmations into Your Pause Plan:

1. **Identify Your "Try" Statements:** Pay attention to where you use hesitant language around rest and self-care.

   ○ *Example:* "I'll try to get to bed earlier tonight."

2. **Transform Them into "I Am" Affirmations:** Rephrase them into clear, positive, present-tense statements. Make them specific and actionable.

   ○ ***Example:*** "I am going to bed at 9 PM tonight to honor my body's need for rest."

   ○ ***Another Example:*** Instead of "I'll try to say no to extra tasks," affirm: "I am confidently setting boundaries to protect my energy."

3. **Repeat and Believe:** Write them down, say them aloud, put them on sticky notes, set them as phone reminders. The more you repeat them with conviction, the more deeply they'll sink into your subconscious. Visualize yourself embodying these affirmations. Feel the peace and power they bring.

- ○ *Examples of powerful Pause Affirmations:*
  - ■ "I am worthy of rest and peace."
  - ■ "I am creating a schedule that supports my well-being."
  - ■ "I am setting healthy boundaries with grace and firmness."
  - ■ "I am prioritizing my mental and physical health daily."
  - ■ "I am fully present in my moments of rest."
  - ■ "I am making time for what truly nourishes my soul."
  - ■ "My worth is not tied to my productivity; my worth is inherent."
  - ■ "I am choosing peace over pressure, every single day."
  - ■ "I am listening to my body's wisdom and honoring its needs."

By shifting from "trying" to "I am," you empower yourself to take decisive action, transforming your intentions into tangible realities. This isn't just about positive thinking; it's about intentional doing, fueled by a belief in your capacity to create the life you truly desire.

The Retirement Paradox: When the Body Keeps Score

We often spend decades in careers that demand a certain pace, a certain level of activity, and a relentless "on" switch. Our bodies adapt to this, becoming conditioned to the daily grind, the constant movement, the mental exertion. So, what happens when that suddenly stops? The common narrative around retirement is blissful relaxation, endless leisure, and freedom from obligation. And while that's certainly a part of it, there's a lesser-known, and frankly, alarming paradox many people face.

Research suggests that for some individuals, the period immediately following retirement can be a time of increased health risks, including a higher incidence of strokes. Why? Because a body that has been conditioned for 25, 30, or even 40 years to a demanding schedule—whether it's physical labor, intense mental problem-solving, or constant social interaction—can react negatively to a sudden, drastic drop in activity. It's as if the system, suddenly without its accustomed "work," struggles to recalibrate. The physical and mental conditioning that once served the demands of work now has nowhere to go, and the sudden shift to a sedentary lifestyle can be dangerous.

This highlights a crucial point: the pause isn't just about recovering from immediate exhaustion; it's about cultivating a sustainable rhythm for your *entire* life. It's about recognizing that your body keeps score—not just of the stress you accumulate, but also of the habits you maintain. If you transition from a highly active work life to a completely inactive retirement, that sudden change can be a shock to your system, leading to serious health consequences. This underscores the importance of planning for well-being throughout all phases of life, ensuring that even in retirement, you maintain a rhythm that honors your body's need for movement, engagement, and purposeful rest, rather than a complete cessation of activity. The toll it puts on your body is dangerous and a stark reminder that proactive self-care is a lifelong commitment.

The idea of waiting until retirement to truly live, to finally rest, is a dangerous one. Life's demands don't magically disappear at 65 and the habits of a lifetime are hard to break. In fact, studies show that the transition to retirement can even come with its own health risks. For instance, research from the Harvard School of Public Health indicates that retirees, especially in their first year, can be **40% more likely to experience a heart attack or stroke** compared to those still working. Other studies, like a prospective analysis of the US Health and Retirement Study, found that being retired was associated with elevated odds of cardiovascular disease (CVD) onset. These findings highlight that, while retirement can offer relief, the abrupt shift can also be a significant stressor. This is precisely why sustainable rhythms matter now, not just in some distant future retirement. Building your pause practice today ensures you're living a full, vibrant life, rather than just waiting for it to begin and proactively safeguarding your well-being.

Footnotes for this section:

1. Kathleen Coxwell, "Heart Health and Your Retirement Well Being," *Boldin*, November 7, 2024.

2. Gang Chen, et al., "Transition to retirement and risk of cardiovascular disease: Prospective analysis of the US Health and Retirement Study," *BMC Public Health* 12, no. 1 (2012): 364.

Rewriting the Hustle Narrative

I used to wake up every morning with the mindset of "rise and grind." I'd even go on social media and post a quote, hashtagged with those very words. It was like a badge of honor, proving how hard I was working or how many hours I was putting in each day. It seemed like a betrayal to prioritize rest if I perceived a never-ending to-do list of "must-dos" wasn't done. I also struggled delegating because I wanted to be sure things were done and done to my standards. Which meant I often missed gatherings with family and friends, turned down invitations, and filled in time that should have been for my social life by adding more work and community meetings and events to my daily calendar. Some days I didn't know if I was coming or going.

I used to take a lot of naps, thinking they were helping, when in reality, if I had been getting the proper amount of rest, they wouldn't have been necessary. There were days I would look up and realize it was almost dinner time and I hadn't eaten all day. I had to rewrite these narratives because I realized this wasn't sustainable. If I wanted to be physically, mentally, emotionally, professionally, and spiritually healthy, something had to change.

I was experiencing a phenomenon known as high-functioning depression, where you keep yourself busy and working nonstop. Still, you're not happy and you're extremely stressed, all while being fatigued, irritable, frustrated, and when not working, distancing yourself from family, friends, and activities that once brought you joy. I had to recognize this in myself, but I couldn't do it on my own. While I lean on my faith, God also gave me good sense, which I used to seek out professional help in the form of a therapist. I LOVE HER. Like, literally, she has probably saved my life. She calls me out, gives me assignments, listens without judgment, and provides the best insight and counsel.

This journey hasn't been about abandoning ambition; it's about redefining success on my own terms. It's about recognizing that true strength isn't measured by how much I do, but by how well I am. I've learned that rest isn't the opposite of work; it's what makes work and life sustainable and meaningful. And that's a narrative worth living and sharing.

Finding Your Rhythm

There's a certain feeling...a sense of being completely in sync with myself, my purpose, and my Creator. It's not something that happens all the time, but when it does, it's like everything just flows. It's a feeling I chase, because when I'm there, I'm my best self. It's a feeling of coming home to myself.

I've found that I'm most in that rhythm when I'm really intentional about a few things. First, it's about protecting my time and schedule. That means saying "no" when I need to and not feeling guilty about it. It's about recognizing that my time is a precious resource and I need to guard it fiercely.

I've learned that overcommitting leads to chaos and that saying no is an act of self-preservation.

It's also about taking care of my physical health. For me, that looks like preparing balanced meals and making exercise a daily priority. It's about honoring my body and giving it the fuel and movement it needs to thrive. And it definitely means not burning the midnight oil every night! Getting to bed at a reasonable hour is key. This isn't just about looking good; it's about feeling good, from the inside out.

My spiritual practices also play a huge role. That means praying before bed and upon rising in the morning. It's about starting and ending my day with gratitude and connection. I also find daily meditations from "My Daily Bread" to be incredibly grounding and centering. And honestly, taking a break from feeling the need to be so connected to social media helps me to quiet the noise and tune into what truly matters. It's a way to disconnect from the external world and reconnect with my inner voice.

When I'm living like this, it's not just about being productive or efficient. It's about living with intention, purpose, and a deep sense of connection to something larger than myself. It's about feeling aligned, whole, and at peace. It's a feeling I hold onto, a feeling I strive to return to, because it's when I feel most truly alive. It's not just a feeling; it's a state of being. It's when I feel most like myself, most authentic, and most connected to the person I was created to be.

Finding your rhythm is about intentional scheduling and protecting your time. For example, in my current week, my calendar already has at least three meetings scheduled each day. My goal is not to go above that limit. This allows me to avoid spending all evening catching up on emails, phone calls, reports, and all the other tasks that accumulate. Because a recent request was not of immediate urgency, I had to—and yes, I mean *had* to—offer a meeting for the following week. This is an active choice to maintain balance and prevent overwhelm.

HOW TO KNOW IT'S TIME TO PAUSE

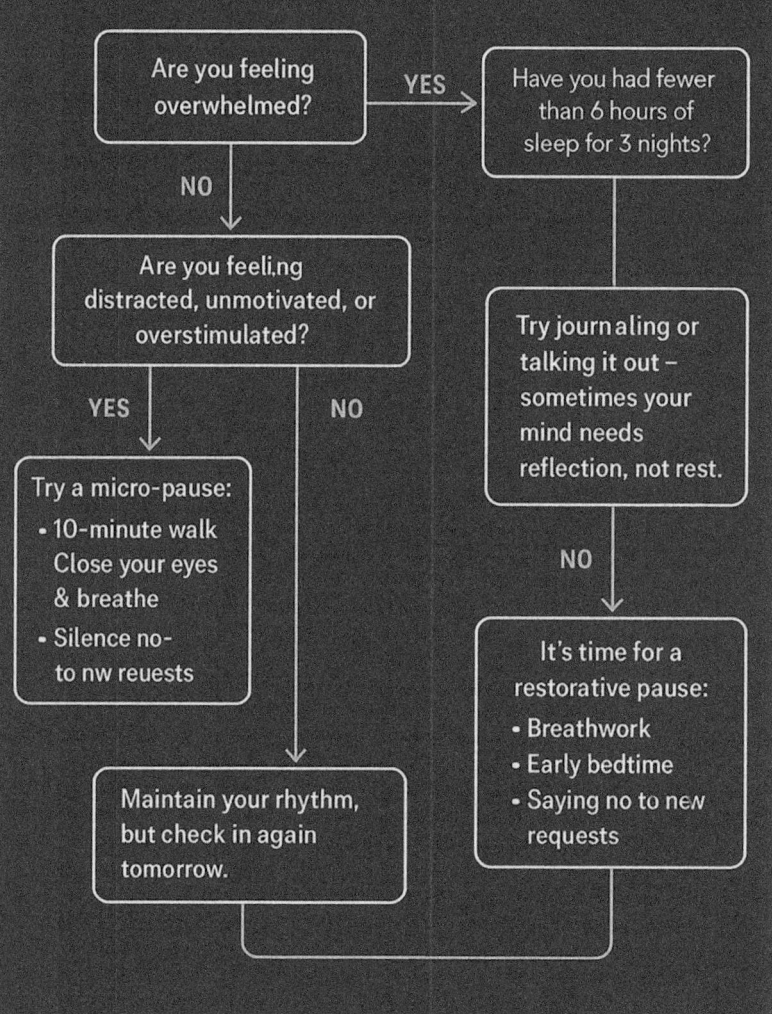

Are you feeling overwhelmed?

— YES →

Have you had fewer than 6 hours of sleep for 3 nights?

NO ↓

Are you feeling distracted, unmotivated, or overstimulated?

YES ↓   NO ↓

Try journaling or talking it out – sometimes your mind needs reflection, not rest.

NO ↓

Try a micro-pause:
- 10-minute walk Close your eyes & breathe
- Silence no- to nw reuests

It's time for a restorative pause:
- Breathwork
- Early bedtime
- Saying no to new requests

Maintain your rhythm, but check in again tomorrow.

Navigating the Realities of Your Pause Plan: Overcoming Hurdles

Creating a pause plan on paper is one thing; consistently implementing it in the messy reality of daily life is another. It's easy to feel enthusiastic when you're designing your ideal rhythm, but the true test comes when external pressures mount or old habits try to pull you back. This is where we need to be both strategic and compassionate with ourselves.

1. **Dealing with External Pressure:** The Art of the Graceful "No"

   The world doesn't always understand or immediately respect your new boundaries. Colleagues might still send late-night emails, friends might expect you to be available for every spontaneous outing, and family might unintentionally encroach on your designated rest time. This isn't a personal attack; it's often just a reflection of their conditioning and expectations. Your job isn't to justify your need for rest, but to communicate your boundaries clearly and consistently.

   - Practical Tips:

     o **Be Proactive:** Inform key people about your new rhythms. For example, "I'm now dedicating my evenings to personal time, so I'll respond to emails during work hours."

- ○ **Use "I" Statements:** Frame your boundaries around your needs, not their demands. "I need to protect my evenings to recharge," rather than "You're asking too much."

- ○ **Offer Alternatives (if appropriate):** "I can't make it to that late-night meeting, but I'm happy to jump on a call first thing in the morning."

- ○ **Short and Sweet:** You don't owe anyone a lengthy explanation. "That sounds lovely, but I won't be able to make it," is perfectly sufficient.

- ○ **Practice, Practice, Practice:** Saying "no" can feel uncomfortable at first, especially if you're a people pleaser. Rehearse your responses, and remember that protecting your peace allows you to show up more fully when you *do* say "yes."

2. **Internal Sabotage:** Quieting the Inner Critic
Even when external pressures are managed, the loudest voice of sabotage often comes from within. That nagging voice that whispers, "You're being lazy," "You should be doing more," "You're falling behind." This

internal critic is often a reflection of deeply ingrained societal messages about productivity and worth.

- Strategies for Quieting the Critic:

  - **Acknowledge, Don't Engage:** When the thought arises, simply acknowledge it ("I hear that thought") but don't get into a debate with it. Let it pass like a cloud.

  - **Counter with Affirmations:** This is where the power of "I am" statements truly shines. Actively replace negative self-talk with your chosen affirmations: "My worth is not tied to my productivity; my worth is inherent."

  - **Remind Yourself of the "Why":** Reconnect with your core reasons for embracing the pause. Remember the burnout, the exhaustion, the desire for a more fulfilling life. This "why" is your fuel.

  - **Self-Compassion:** Treat yourself with the same kindness and understanding you would offer a dear friend. Would you tell a friend they're lazy for needing rest? Probably not. Extend that same grace to yourself.

3. **Consistency Over Perfection:** Getting Back on Track
No one's pause plan will be perfectly executed every single day. Life happens. Unexpected demands arise. You might miss a planned ritual or fall back into old habits. The key is not to let a slip-up derail your entire journey.

- Embracing Imperfection:

  o **Forgive Yourself Quickly:** Don't dwell on missed moments. Acknowledge it, learn from it, and move on. Guilt is a heavy backpack you don't need to carry.

  o **One Small Step:** If you've fallen off track, don't try to immediately implement your entire plan. Just pick one small, manageable pause for the day or the next hour. A mindful breath, a five-minute stretch. Build momentum from there.

  o **Review and Adjust:** Regularly (perhaps weekly or monthly) review your pause plan. What worked? What didn't? What needs tweaking? Your rhythm will evolve, and your plan should too.

  o **Celebrate Small Wins:** Acknowledge every time you successfully implement a pause, no matter how small. This positive reinforcement builds momentum and makes the practice more enjoyable.

By anticipating these common hurdles and having strategies in place, you can navigate the path to a sustainable rhythm with greater ease and resilience. Your pause plan isn't a rigid rulebook; it's a living document, designed to support your evolving well-being.

Reflection Prompts for Chapter 3: Creating Your Pause Plan

- What are your top three energy leaks—and how can you plug them?

- Describe a time you said 'no' and it saved your peace.

- What does a sustainable week look like for you now?

- Create a boundary script for when you're tempted to overcommit.

- What's a rhythm or routine that feeds your soul—not just your schedule?

- What are the signs you're living by someone else's definition of success?

CHAPTER 4

Solo Serenity

The medicine of solitude, learning to enjoy your own company

Solo Serenity

In a world that constantly encourages connection and collaboration, the idea of solitude can feel counterintuitive, even isolating. Yet, it is in deliberate alone time that we discover profound self-awareness, deep restoration, and the quiet joy of our own company. Solitude is not loneliness; it is a chosen sanctuary.

My journey into solo serenity began with small, deliberate steps. The first was the humble solo dinner. For years, I'd avoided eating alone, feeling self-conscious, as if it proclaimed my lack of social connection. But one evening, feeling depleted and craving simplicity, I decided to treat myself to a quiet meal at a favorite restaurant. No distractions, no conversation, just me and my thoughts, savoring each bite. It was unexpectedly liberating. The world didn't end. In fact, I felt a gentle peace settle over me. Table for one please!

This small act of self-compassion paved the way for a more significant venture: a solo trip to Seattle. Why Seattle, you ask? It wasn't my choice at all! This was a surprise vacation curated by a company called "Pack Up N Go." I literally did not know my destination or any of the activities until the day I left. That's right, completely in the dark until departure! Friends and family questioned my choice – "Aren't you worried you'll be lonely?" or "Why not go with someone?" But I felt an undeniable pull to experience a new city completely on my own terms. I wandered through Pike Place Market at my own pace, lingered in quiet cafes, and spent time on daily excursions without the pressure to entertain or compromise. It was on that trip that I truly understood the difference between loneliness and solitude. Loneliness is an unwanted feeling of isolation; solitude is a chosen, restorative state of being alone. Seattle became my testament to the profound healing and self-discovery that can unfold when we embrace our own company. It was a space where I could hear my thoughts, unedited, and rediscover who I was, separate from my roles and relationships. This journey, initially born out of necessity to heal from burnout, became a cherished practice of self-nourishment.

I love my alone time—hell, I take myself out to dinner, table for one! There's no pressure for small talk and I can just enjoy my own company. Don't get me wrong, I'm a very social person, but there are times when my social battery runs low. But I love me; I'm a great date (insert sarcasm here).

I used to feel like I always needed people around me to have fun or to make something feel special. If I were planning an outing, my first thought was always, "Who can I invite?" It was almost as if an experience wasn't truly valid or enjoyable unless it was shared. But I learned that's just not so. I discovered that moments can be incredibly rich and meaningful just by experiencing them myself. It's amazing how much more you notice, how much more deeply you feel, when you're not splitting your attention. You can truly savor a meal, get lost in a book, or simply appreciate the quiet beauty of a walk, without any external expectations. Solitude isn't about being isolated; it's about being in your own company, and sometimes, that's the best company you can keep. It's where I can truly hear myself think, feel, and just be. Turns out, I am a good damn time!

I remember one particular evening, I had tickets to a concert that a friend had to cancel on last minute. My first instinct was to try to find someone else to go with, or even just sell the ticket. But something in me, that quiet voice I've learned to listen to, said, "Just go. Go by yourself." And I did. I got there, found my seat, and for the first time, I wasn't worried about making conversation or if the other person was enjoying themselves. I just listened to the music. I felt the energy of the crowd, but from my own peaceful center. It was incredibly liberating. That night, the music resonated with me on a deeper level than it ever had before, because my focus was entirely inward. It was a profound healing experience, realizing that joy and connection don't always require another person's presence; sometimes, they just require your own.

And it's not just big events. It's the small moments, too. I've found immense healing in simply sitting by myself, watching the rain, or enjoying a cup of coffee in silence before the house wakes up. There's a particular comfort in knowing that I don't need external validation or company to make a moment special. These quiet times allow me to process thoughts, to feel emotions without judgment, and to simply exist without the need to perform or entertain. It's in these moments of solo serenity that I truly recharge, reconnect with my inner self, and find a deep sense of peace that carries me through the more social aspects of my life.

The healing that happened on that trip, simply by being present with myself, was profound. It taught me that my own company is more than enough to make any moment or trip truly special. When you learn to be with yourself, you also learn not to chase people, noise, or obligations just to fill the silence. You give yourself space to heal, reflect, and grow. It's not about isolation; it's about deep self-trust.

When the World Expects You to Keep Going

One of the hardest aspects of embracing solitude is the societal expectation to always be "on" and connected. After a major life event or even a simple vacation, the world expects us to jump right back into the fray, no questions asked. There's little cultural space for sustained periods of introspection or quiet integration.

I remember returning from that Seattle trip, feeling deeply refreshed, but immediately faced with the onslaught of emails and demands. It took a conscious effort to resist the pull to revert to my old pace, to protect the newfound peace I'd cultivated. Learning to say "no" to immediate re-engagement and carve out soft landings after intense periods is a vital part of sustained well-being.

There are those times when everything around you is screaming, "Keep going! Don't stop!" The demands of work, community, and life create this relentless pressure to move, produce, and be doing all the time. I found myself in that space not too long ago. I was getting dangerously close to hitting my wall. My social battery was constantly running on fumes, and I was juggling work around the clock with a slew of community commitments. I was stretched thin and knew I couldn't keep going at that pace.

I had an international trip planned, but when the plans fell through, it felt like a strange twist of fate. I still had the time off on my calendar, and that's when a different possibility presented itself. It was as if the universe was saying, "Here's your chance." So, I took a leap of faith and booked my first-ever solo vacation—a decision I know I will repeat.

A colleague had told me about a travel company called Pack Up N Go. They offer these surprise vacations; they'll book trips for 1-10 people, anywhere from 3-10 days. The crazy part is, you don't know where you're going until the day of your trip! You fill out a questionnaire, and based on your answers, they curate this personalized experience. They ask about cities you've been to, upcoming travel plans, and places you have no desire to visit. They inquire about your preferred travel activities and whether you want to support BIPOC businesses.

I booked my trip about three weeks before departure. I received an email with my departure time and some suggested packing items, along with a weather forecast. About a week before I was set to leave, I got a packet in the mail with instructions not to open it until the morning of my travel. Based on the weather forecast and the hints in the email, I started guessing I was headed somewhere in the Pacific Northwest, especially since they suggested packing a travel pillow, indicating a longer flight than their usual trips from Wisconsin. My curiosity was definitely piqued. I wanted to know what to pack, so at 2 AM on the day of my travel, I gave in and opened the packet. (Of course, I made a cute video to share on social media!) Inside, I found out I was going to Seattle!

The envelope contained my hotel information, a detailed itinerary, an Uber gift card, gift cards for two of the four restaurants where they'd made reservations, and passes for all my excursions. They really nailed it. I'd told them I was a foodie and loved being near the water, and they set me up with amazing restaurants and a harbor boat cruise. I also visited the Space Needle and the Chihuly Garden and Glass exhibit. The packet even included three pages of other attractions and restaurants I might enjoy. It was all so perfectly planned. For those five days, I got something I desperately needed: rest. I never even opened my laptop. I was able to completely relax, eat well, explore at my own pace, and, most importantly, just be. I came back from that trip with a renewed sense of energy and a pep in my step, ready to take on the world again, but also with the wisdom to know that I didn't have to take it all on at once. That trip was a powerful reminder that sometimes, the most productive thing you can do is stop. It wasn't easy to choose rest, but it was necessary. It was a gift, and it taught me that I am worth it.

Graceful Exits and Firm "No": Navigating Social Boundaries

The desire to be liked, to be a team player, or to avoid awkwardness can often lead us to overcommit socially, even when our internal battery is flashing red. Learning to navigate social expectations with grace, while firmly protecting your peace, is a crucial skill for solo serenity. It's not about being rude or isolating yourself; it's about being intentional with your precious social energy.

- **Recognize Your "Tells":** Before you even leave the house, or as you step into an event, pay attention to your body's signals. Do you feel a sense of dread? Is your energy already low? These are your internal cues telling you to be strategic.

- **Pre-Plan Your Escape:** If you know an event might be draining, decide beforehand how long you'll stay and what your exit strategy will be. "I'm just stopping by for an hour," or "I have an early start tomorrow," are perfectly valid reasons.

- **The Power of the Polite Decline:** You don't need a dramatic excuse. Simple, firm, and polite "nos" are your best friends.
  - "Thank you so much for the invitation, but I won't be able to make it." (No explanation needed!)
  - "I appreciate you thinking of me, but I need to protect my rest time this week."
  - "That sounds wonderful, but I'm focusing on a quieter pace right now."

- **Delegate Social Labor (Your "Armor Bearer"):** As we discussed, having a trusted friend or partner who understands your needs can be invaluable. This person can help divert conversations, create an opening for your exit, or simply act as a buffer when you're feeling overwhelmed. A quick glance or a pre-arranged signal can communicate volumes without a word.

- **Embrace the Joy of Missing Out (JOMO):** Instead of FOMO, cultivate JOMO. Find genuine pleasure in the quiet moments you gain by choosing rest. Celebrate the peace, the personal time, and the energy you preserve. When you truly enjoy your solitude, the pull of external social demands lessens significantly.

- **Prioritize Quality Over Quantity:** It's better to have a few deeply nourishing social interactions than a calendar packed with draining obligations. Choose connections that uplift and energize you and gently release those that consistently deplete your battery.

Navigating social landscapes requires self-awareness and courage. By consciously setting and maintaining social boundaries, you empower yourself to truly enjoy your solo serenity and engage more authentically when you *do* choose to connect.

Reflections on the Difference between Loneliness and Solitude

This distinction is critical. Loneliness often feels empty, a yearning for connection that is absent. It can be painful and isolating. Solitude, on the other hand, feels full, a rich inner landscape where creativity, clarity, and self-understanding can flourish. It is a conscious choice to withdraw from external demands to reconnect with oneself. Loneliness is a void; solitude is a sanctuary. One depletes, the other restores.

Reflection Prompts for Chapter 4: Solo Serenity

- What have you learned about yourself in moments of solitude?

- Describe your ideal solo day—hour by hour.

- What does it mean to enjoy your own company?

- Write about a moment you felt God meet you in solitude.

- What fear or resistance do you feel about being alone?

CHAPTER 5

Crafting Your Pause Ritual

Designing routines for rest and joy

Self-Care Is The Best Care

"Self-care is the best care." This isn't just a catchy phrase; it's a profound truth that I've come to live by—and it's one we absolutely need to embrace if we want to show up fully in our lives. We need to take care of ourselves, because if we don't care for ourselves, we are no good to those who rely on us. Think about it: you can't pour from an empty cup. If you're constantly depleted, running on fumes, and neglecting your needs, how can you genuinely support your family, excel in your work, or be a present friend? Prioritizing your well-being isn't selfish; it's foundational. It's the most responsible thing you can do for yourself and everyone in your life.

Self-care shows up in countless ways and it doesn't always have to be a grand gesture or an expensive spa day (though those are wonderful too!). It's about intentionally choosing activities that replenish your physical, mental, emotional, and spiritual reserves. It's about recognizing your unique needs and honoring them.

Ways to Give Yourself Self-Care:

Self-care is deeply personal, but here are some categories and examples to inspire your practice:

- **Physical Self-Care:** This focuses on nurturing your body.

  - **Movement as Medicine:** As simple as taking a walk to clear your mind, doing gentle stretches, dancing to your favorite song, or engaging in a full workout. The goal is to move your body in a way that feels good and energizing. Sometimes pausing doesn't mean lying down—it means moving intentionally. Gentle movement—like yoga, a long walk, or even dancing in your living room—can release stored stress and emotions. The key is not exertion for calorie burn, but movement for emotional and energetic release.

○ **Nourishment:** Eating balanced, wholesome meals that fuel your body. This also includes allowing yourself to enjoy comfort foods mindfully, without guilt. Identify a few go-to comfort foods that nourish both body and soul (e.g., homemade soup, a favorite warm drink). Prepare them mindfully, savoring the process.

○ **Sleep:** Prioritizing consistent, restorative sleep. This includes creating a conducive sleep environment and a relaxing bedtime routine. Reframe naps as power-ups, not signs of weakness. Even 20 minutes can significantly improve alertness and mood.

○ **Hydration:** Consistently drinking enough water throughout the day.

○ **Pampering:** Taking yourself for a massage, a pedicure, a long warm bath, or simply moisturizing your skin. These acts acknowledge and appreciate your physical vessel.

- **Mental Self-Care:** This involves stimulating your mind in healthy ways and managing mental fatigue.

  - **Mindfulness and Meditation:** Practices like mindful breathing, sensory check-ins, or guided meditations to bring you into the present moment and calm a racing mind.

  - **Learning and Creativity:** Reading a book for pleasure, learning a new skill, engaging in a hobby like painting, writing, or playing an instrument.

  - **Digital Detox:** Setting boundaries around screen time, especially from social media and news, to reduce mental clutter and overstimulation. Implement "no-phone zones" (bedroom, dinner table) and scheduled "screen-free hours" daily. Use app timers to limit social media.

  - **Problem-Solving:** Dedicating specific time to tackle a nagging problem, rather than letting it linger and create mental stress.

- **Emotional Self-Care:** This is about acknowledging and processing your feelings in a healthy way.

- ○ **Journaling:** Writing down your thoughts and emotions to gain clarity and release pent-up feelings.

- ○ **Seeking Support:** Talking to a trusted friend, family member, or therapist about what you're experiencing.

- ○ **Expressing Creativity:** Using art, music, or writing as an outlet for emotional expression.

- ○ **Setting Boundaries:** Protecting your emotional energy by saying "no" to draining requests or interactions. Learning to say "no" graciously but firmly. Communicating your availability clearly to others. Protecting your non-negotiable pause times.

- **Spiritual Self-Care:** This connects you to your sense of purpose, meaning, or a higher power.

- ○ **Prayer and Reflection:** Engaging in spiritual practices that resonate with you, like prayer, meditation, or reading inspirational texts.

- ○ **Time in Nature:** Spending time outdoors, connecting with the natural world.

- ○ **Acts of Service:** Giving back to your community in a way that feels meaningful and fulfilling.

- ○ **Practicing Gratitude:** Regularly acknowledging the blessings in your life.

- **Social Self-Care:** This is about nurturing your relationships and ensuring your social interactions are replenishing, not draining.

  - ○ **Meaningful Connections:** Spending quality time with people who uplift and support you.

  - ○ **Setting Social Boundaries:** Knowing when to say "no" to social engagements when your social battery is low.

  - ○ **Alone Time:** Embracing solitude when needed to recharge, as discussed in the "Solo Serenity" chapter.

The key is to experiment and discover what truly replenishes you. Self-care isn't a luxury; it's a necessity. It's the fuel that allows you to live a vibrant, purposeful life and be present for yourself and for those you love.

Anatomy of a Mental Health Day

The perfect mental health day can look a number of different ways. It could be as simple as vegging out on the couch, watching mindless TV, and eating your favorite snacks, or as extravagant as having a spa day with a massage, facial, and other pampering. It could be as simple as a trip to the nail salon to get a manicure and/or pedicure, or as extravagant as a staycation at a local hotel. So long as you put yourself first, turn off the work notifications, emails, and calls. Put your phone on "do not disturb," and turn on the out-of-office responder on your email. Eat what you want, get dressed, or stay in your pajamas all day. It's your day to enjoy it as you see fit. Having time and peace to yourself is invaluable.

To expand on that, a mental health day is truly about honoring your needs and allowing yourself to step away from the demands of your daily routine. It's a proactive way to prevent burnout, reduce stress, and recharge your mental and emotional batteries. Here are some additional elements you could incorporate into your perfect mental health day:

- **Mindful Morning:** Start your day with a gentle activity that eases you into a relaxed state. This could be light stretching, meditation, journaling, or enjoying a cup of tea in silence.

- **Digital Detox:** Logging Out to Plug In

    o Let's be honest—sometimes we're not just tired, we're overstimulated. Our screens don't just demand our attention, they fracture it. Social media, while beautiful in its ability to connect, often keeps us in a loop of comparison, urgency, and noise. A social media detox isn't about hating technology—it's about reclaiming your peace.

        ■ **Try this strategy:**- Pick a detox window: 24 hours, a weekend, or even one evening a week. Move social apps off your home screen. Use "Do Not Disturb" or Focus Mode after a certain hour. Replace scrolling with stillness—read, breathe, stretch, stare out a window. At first, you may feel restless. That's not boredom—it's withdrawal from overstimulation. Let it pass. Stillness has to be practiced like any other habit.

- **Reconnect with your breath** With your body. With now. You deserve that clarity.

- **Nourishing Your Body:** Enjoy meals that make you feel good, whether it's a healthy home-cooked meal or indulging in your favorite comfort food. The focus is on savoring the experience without guilt or restrictions.

- **Engaging in Joyful Activities:** Spend time doing things you love, whether it's reading a book, listening to music, spending time in nature, pursuing a hobby, or simply relaxing in a warm bath.

- **Setting Boundaries:** Communicate your need for space to loved ones and colleagues. Let them know that you're taking a day to focus on yourself and will be unavailable.

- **Rest and Recharge:** Allow yourself to rest without feeling guilty. Take naps, sleep in, or simply lounge around and do nothing.

- **Reflect and Reconnect:** Use this time to reflect on your thoughts, feelings, and needs. You can journal, meditate, or simply sit in quiet contemplation. This can help you gain clarity and a deeper understanding of yourself. The most important aspect of a mental health day is that it's tailored to your individual needs and preferences. There is no one-size-fits-all approach. It's about giving yourself permission to prioritize your well-being and create a day that leaves you feeling refreshed, rejuvenated, and ready to take on the world. This is also where the concept of an "executive break" comes in – it's not just a vacation, but an intentional, often shorter, period designed to clear your mind, strategize, and recharge, ensuring you're operating at your highest capacity without succumbing to burnout. It's a proactive pause for leaders, a strategic withdrawal to gain perspective and renewed energy.

Pajama Power

The power of pajamas is REAL. The comfort of being in your favorite pajamas or robe—I even have a hooded blanket that is the best thing ever. Why get dressed when my plan for the day is to take naps and not move off the couch? In those times, I've been able to reset, refocus, rejuvenate, refresh, and, above all, REST. All are very necessary to help balance this crazy world we live in and the daily stress we encounter in our personal and professional lives. 'Cause life be life-ing, and we need time to step back and get a recharge.

Pajamas symbolize a shedding of pretense and the outside world. They represent a state of being where you're free to be your most authentic self, without the need to perform or adhere to societal expectations. They're soft, loose-fitting, and create a sense of security, signaling to your mind and body that it's time to relax and let go of stress. The choice to stay in pajamas all day is an act of rebellion against the constant pressure to be productive and presentable. It's a way of saying, "My time is mine and I get to decide how I spend it." In our fast-paced world, rest is often undervalued and seen as unproductive. Pajamas give us permission to rest without guilt. They're a physical reminder that it's okay to prioritize our well-being and recharge. There's a vulnerability in staying in your pajamas. It's an acknowledgment that you're not okay and need time to heal and recover. It allows you to process emotions without the pressure of having to put on a brave face. Pajamas are often associated with childhood, a time when we were carefree and unburdened by adult responsibilities. They can evoke a sense of nostalgia and help us reconnect with our inner child, fostering self-compassion and acceptance. A mental health day spent in pajamas can be a powerful act of self-care, a way to create a personal sanctuary where you can nurture your mind, body, and soul, and return to the world feeling renewed and refreshed.

Seasonal Rituals: Farmers Market, Retail Therapy Walks

My self-care shifts with the seasons. In spring and summer, my ritual involves regular visits to the farmers market. The vibrant colors, fresh scents, and sense of community ground me. It's a slow, sensory experience that connects me to nature's rhythm and the simple pleasure of good food. In colder months, "retail therapy walks" (which are more about browsing than buying) through charming local shops offer a different kind of sensory stimulation and a cozy escape from the elements. These rituals are about tuning into the environment and allowing it to inform my need for rest and joy.

And for me, "me time" can also look like specific rituals depending on the season. During the summer months, one of my favorite things to do is go to the farmers market on Saturday mornings. I take my empty backpack and a $20 bill. Then, I just walk, snack on whatever looks good, shop for fresh goodies, and people-watch. Once that $20 is spent, I might hang around and people-watch for a little longer, then I head home and unpack my purchases. It's simple, but it's pure joy. During the winter months, on Sunday evenings, I'll head to one of my favorite retail stores and just walk around, looking at the clearance racks, seeing what deals I can find on essential items. Sometimes I leave empty-handed, sometimes I leave with a bag full of treasures. It's not about the shopping; it's about the quiet time, the hunt, and the simple pleasure of being out and about on my own terms.

The Retail Therapy Story

Here's a little secret about me... I LOVE shoes. Sandals, sneakers, heels, boots—it doesn't matter, I just love shoes. Many times, I start with the shoes, then plan the outfit around them. When I worked in downtown Chicago, my office was a block away from Macy's. If I needed a break or had a stressful moment, I would walk over and go straight to the floor where the shoe clearance section was. I would spend some time trying on shoes, sometimes just window shopping, sometimes I might find a steal of a deal that I just couldn't pass up. Then I would "woosah" and back to work I went. It was my little escape, a quick, personal pause that helped me reset and re-enter the day with a calmer mind. This ritual of mine, whether it's a quiet browse or a thoughtful purchase, isn't just about the item itself. It's part of how I reset; it clears my mind and allows me a moment of intentional focus outside of my usual demands.

These aren't grand gestures, but they are powerful. They are my personal "Selah" moments, where I intentionally hit pause on the relentless rhythm of life. They allow me to truly process, to breathe, and to reconnect with my inner peace and my Creator. It's in these sacred pauses that true rejuvenation happens, allowing me to return to the world not just rested, but deeply refreshed and ready to face whatever comes next.

When Rituals Go Sideways: Embracing Flexibility

Even the most well-intentioned pause rituals can get derailed. Life happens. An unexpected deadline, a sick child, a sudden travel plan, or simply a day when you just don't feel like it can throw your carefully crafted routine off course. The danger here isn't the disruption itself, but the tendency to fall into an "all or nothing" mindset, where one missed ritual leads to abandoning the practice entirely. The key to sustainable pause rituals isn't rigid adherence, but flexible adaptation and self-compassion.

- **Forgive Yourself Immediately:** When you realize you've missed a ritual or fallen off track, offer yourself grace. Guilt and self-criticism are counterproductive; they drain energy and make it harder to get back on track. Acknowledge the slip-up without judgment.

- **Embrace "Micro-Rituals":** On days when a full ritual isn't possible, scale it down. Can you manage just one mindful breath? A 30-second stretch? A single sip of tea savored in silence? Even these tiny moments can serve as anchors and keep the habit alive. The goal is consistency, not perfection of form.

- **Identify the Root Cause:** Briefly reflect on why the ritual was missed. Was it a genuine external disruption? Or was it internal resistance, lack of motivation, or poor planning? Understanding the cause helps you address it proactively next time.

- **Adjust, Don't Abandon:** Your life changes, and so should your rituals. If a particular time or activity consistently isn't working, adjust it. Maybe your morning meditation needs to become an evening one, or your long walk needs to be broken into two shorter ones. Be creative and find what fits your current reality.

- **Re-engage with Intention:** Don't wait for the "perfect" moment to restart. As soon as you can, pick up where you left off. The power is in the intention to return, not in never deviating. Remind yourself of the benefits and gently guide yourself back to the practice.

- **Batch and Stack:** Look for opportunities to combine rituals or stack them with existing habits. Can you listen to calming music while doing a chore? Can your mindful eating happen during a work break? Small integrations can make a big difference.

Remember, the purpose of a pause ritual is to support your well-being, not to add another layer of stress or obligation. Be kind to yourself, be flexible, and trust that even imperfect consistency will lead to profound benefits.

Create Your Own Ritual Worksheet (Sample Prompts)

- **My Go-To Reset Practice:** What is one small thing you can do anytime, anywhere, that instantly helps you feel calmer and more centered? (e.g., threedeep breaths, a sip of water, looking out the window for 30 seconds)

- **My Dream Mental Health Day:** Fill in the blanks with activities that truly nourish you.

  - Wake-up:
  - Morning activity:
  - Lunch:
  - Afternoon activity:
  - Evening wind-down:

- **Sensory Sanctuary:** List sensory experiences that bring you back to yourself.

  - Sight: (e.g., candles, nature view, art)
  - Sound: (e.g., quiet music, nature sounds, silence)
  - Smell: (e.g., essential oils, fresh coffee, rain, favorite perfume/cologne)
  - Touch: (e.g., soft blanket, warm bath, comfortable clothes, smooth stones)
  - Taste: (e.g., herbal tea, dark chocolate, a favorite fruit, a comforting meal)

- **Seasonal/Mood Shifts:** How does your self-care change with:

  - Spring:
  - Summer:
  - Autumn:
  - Winter:
  - When Stressed/Overwhelmed:
  - When Joyful/Energized:

- **My Safety/Wholeness Ritual:** A Core Practice

  - Describe a personal ritual (new or old) that consistently makes you feel safe, seen, or whole.

What are its key elements? This is your anchor, your reliable go-to.

Reflecting on Your Journey to Pause: Consider your past experiences and how they shaped your relationship with rest.

- What messages did you receive about "pausing" or "rest" when you were younger? How did these experiences condition your beliefs about productivity versus rest?

- How do these past beliefs compare and contrast with what you are learning and choosing to believe about pausing now?

- If you could offer your younger self advice about the importance of pausing, what would it be?

Pause Plan Continuity: Use this worksheet to reflect on how rest looks and works best for you.

- What are my go-to pause rituals?

- What does rest look like in this season of my life?

- How do I know when I'm nearing depletion?

- What does my "emergency rest reset" plan look like?

- How can I protect these rhythms when life gets full again?

Reflection Prompts for Chapter 5: Crafting Your Pause Ritual

- What small practice always helps you reset, no matter what?

- Design your dream mental health day from wake to sleep.

- What sensory experiences (sight, sound, smell) bring you back to yourself?

- How does your self-care shift by season or mood?

- Describe a ritual that made you feel safe, seen, or whole.

CHAPTER 6

The Afterglow

Legacy, impact, sustainability

Leaning into Legacy

When we choose a life of intentional pause and presence, we are not only enriching our existence but also subtly shaping the world around us. Our legacy isn't just about what we build or achieve, but how we live. It's about the quality of our presence, the compassion we offer, and the example we set. Leaning into legacy means consciously asking: "What quiet wisdom do I want to impart? What kind of energy do I want to leave behind?" It's a shift from striving for external recognition to cultivating an inner richness that naturally overflows and inspires.

When I look at my Divine Seven list—that snapshot of a moment in 2020 during shelter-in-place—I see how my commitment to pausing, dreaming, and recalibrating has truly shaped how those visions have unfolded. It wasn't just a list of goals; it was a declaration of hope for ventures I wanted to pursue when the world opened up again. My passions were pulling me in different directions: education, entrepreneurship, and food. They all stem from a core desire to connect with people, build community, and share my gifts.

The interesting part is that I didn't check things off one by one. Life had its own plans. My holiday-themed digital cookbook was a labor of love in 2020, connecting with my passion for food and providing value during a challenging time. In 2021, I started a photo booth business, a leap that allowed me to create fun and memorable experiences. My food demonstrations evolved organically on social media, becoming an unexpected way to share my passion.

While the food hall and event space didn't materialize as brick-and-mortar locations, a career shift in 2022 led me to become the executive director of a marketplace. This was a plot twist where those visions morphed into a different expression, allowing me to support local food vendors and build a vibrant community space, which was my original desire.

Those pauses, those moments of recalibration, have been crucial. If I hadn't learned to step back, rest, and listen to that inner voice, I wouldn't have had the clarity or energy to see and pursue these opportunities sustainably. The photo booth business could have burned me out if I hadn't learned boundaries and delegation. The marketplace role came from being open to change, which I might have missed if I were still running on empty. My social media food demonstrations thrive because I bring my whole, rested self to them, connecting authentically with joy and enthusiasm. The cookbook was a product of having the time and space to be creative and pour my heart into something meaningful.

This journey has taught me that the Divine Seven dreams are a compass, not checkboxes. It's okay if the path isn't straight. It's about staying true to the vision, adapting, pivoting, pausing, and trusting that every step is part of a bigger plan.

The Strength of Softness

Our culture often equates strength with relentless pushing, with being hard and unyielding. But the true power of the pause reveals a different kind of strength: the strength of softness. It's the resilience that comes from rest, the clarity born of stillness, the wisdom found in listening.

Softness isn't weakness; it's adaptability, empathy, and the profound capacity for gentleness with oneself and others. It is a strength that endures, that heals, and leads to a more sustainable and fulfilling way of being. Embracing softness allows us to bend without breaking, to flow with life's currents rather than rigidly resisting them.

I used to believe in the "never let 'em see you sweat" mentality, suppressing vulnerability and putting on a brave face. This constant striving for hardness was exhausting, taking immense energy to bottle up emotions and maintain an impenetrable exterior. But pausing taught me a different way: the tremendous strength in allowing ourselves to be vulnerable, authentic, and to embrace our true selves. This "hard exterior" is exhausting and prevents true connection and experiencing the full range of human emotions.

When we allow ourselves to be soft, we give permission to acknowledge and process emotions healthily. We learn to set healthy boundaries, communicate needs without guilt, and ask for help, recognizing we don't have to do it all alone. This softness fosters authentic connection, deeper relationships, and self-compassion. In a world that equates strength with toughness, embracing softness is radical and courageous, but it's where we find our true power.

Future Gratitude Letter

One powerful exercise in envisioning this afterglow is writing a "Future Gratitude Letter." Imagine yourself 10, 20, or even 30 years from now, looking back on your life. What are you profoundly grateful for? This isn't about wishing for things; it's about acknowledging the gifts that unfolded because you chose the path of the pause. It might be the deepened relationships, the creative endeavors finally pursued, the peace you cultivated, or the unexpected opportunities that arose from a life lived at a more humane pace. This letter becomes a guiding star, reminding you of the enduring value of your present choices.

Here's a letter to your 60-year-old self, incorporating the themes we've explored in your writing:

Future Gratitude: A Letter to My 60-Year-Old Self

Dearest Future Me,

As I sit here today, in this moment of reflection and growth, my heart is filled with a profound sense of gratitude for the woman you have become. I'm writing to thank you, from the depths of my being, for the choices you've made, the battles you've fought, and the life you've courageously lived.

Thank you for choosing rest. Thank you for listening to that inner voice, the one that whispered even when the world was screaming, "Keep going!" I know there were times when the pressure to hustle, grind, and prove your worth through endless activity must have been immense. There were probably moments when you felt guilty for slowing down, for prioritizing your well-being over the demands of a relentless world. But you did it. You chose rest. And in doing so, you chose life. You chose sustainability. You chose yourself.

I hope you look back on those moments of stillness, not with regret, but with a deep sense of pride. Because in those pauses, in those moments of quiet reflection, you found clarity. You found strength. You found the courage to keep going, not in a frenzied rush, but with intention and purpose.

Thank you for pushing through the doubt. I know that voice well – the one that whispers insecurities, the one that questions your path, the one that tries to hold you back with fear. There were times when you questioned your ability, worthiness, and your calling. You faced setbacks, disappointments, and moments of profound uncertainty. But you didn't let doubt define you. You pushed through. You sought help when needed. You leaned on your faith, your community, and your inner wisdom. And you emerged stronger, more resilient, and more deeply connected to your truth.

Thank you for living a life true to your calling. I know that calling has evolved over the years, taking you down unexpected paths and leading you to places you never imagined. You embraced the detours, the plot twists, the moments when the map was unclear. You allowed your passions to guide you, even when they seemed to defy logic or convention. You created, you connected, you built community, and you shared your gifts with the world, in your own unique and authentic way.

At 60, I hope you are surrounded by love, joy, and a deep sense of fulfillment. I hope you are still taking those solo trips, still laughing with friends, still savoring delicious meals, and still finding magic in the everyday moments. I hope you have learned to fully embrace the strength in softness, the power of vulnerability, and the beauty of a life lived in rhythm with your soul.

Most of all, I hope you know, deep in your heart, that every choice you made, every step you took, every moment of rest and every moment of courage, has led you to this beautiful, rich, and meaningful life.

Love Always,
Your Younger Self

Divine Seven Vision

The "Divine Seven Vision" is a framework for ensuring your life is balanced and nourished across key dimensions. It involves identifying seven core areas of your life (e.g., Spiritual, Physical, Mental, Emotional, Relational, Vocational, Financial) and envisioning what flourishing looks like in each, guided by your redefined sense of success and the power of the pause. This vision isn't about perfection, but about intentional growth and sustainability in all areas, ensuring that no single aspect is neglected at the expense of another. It helps create a holistic afterglow that radiates from within.

Breath Prayer for Breakthrough

In moments of challenge or when seeking clarity for the future, a simple "breath prayer" can be a powerful tool for breakthrough.

- **Inhale:** Silently repeat a word or phrase that represents what you want to invite in (e.g., "Peace," "Clarity," "Courage").

- **Exhale:** Silently repeat a word or phrase that represents what you want to release (e.g., "Fear," "Busyness," "Doubt").

This rhythmic practice connects your breath to your intention, creating a sacred space for transformation and breakthrough, anchoring you in the present while gently guiding you towards your desired future.

Here's a breath prayer for breakthrough, incorporating the elements you described:

Breath Prayer for Breakthrough

Source of all that is, I anchor myself in You.

(Inhale)

I choose faith, even when I cannot see the path.

(Exhale)

I overflow with gratitude for the abundance that surrounds me and for the blessings seen and unseen.

(Inhale)

Grant me discernment, that I may walk in wisdom and truth, and direct my steps according to Your purpose.

(Exhale)

I pray for strength and wholeness in my mind, body, and spirit.

Mend what is broken, and renew me from the inside out.

(Inhale)

I thank you in advance for the victories and breakthroughs in this season, knowing that you are with me in every moment.

(Exhale)

Even for those who may oppose me, I extend a hand of blessing. May they find healing, understanding, and peace.

(Inhale)

I am resilient. I am worthy. I am held.

(Exhale)

Your love sustains me.

Leading the Pause: Organizational Commitment to Rest

This section is not just about a concept; it's about the ripple effect of your journey. Leading the Pause is a core part of my legacy—a commitment to inspire others to find their essential moments of rest and reflection, creating a healthier, more present world, one pause at a time.

You know, I've been so incredibly inspired by some of my community colleagues—true leaders and organizations who don't just talk about work-life balance, but actually live it and bake it into their culture. I've seen out-of-office messages that say things like:

- "At XXXX, we believe a healthy work-life balance is essential to building a thriving team and community. To honor this commitment, our offices will be closed the week of Independence Day, from June 30 through July 4. We look forward to reconnecting with our partners and community on July 7, reenergized and ready to continue advancing our shared work."

- And another one that truly resonated with me: "The XXX is committed to 'Be Well' respite time for employees during this holiday season. The Foundation staff will be offline from December 22nd through January 1st. Our staff are taking this needed time to recharge and look forward to returning on January 2nd. We look forward to replying to your inquiry upon our return."

- And here's another fantastic example I've seen: "Thank you for your email, our office is closed for the gift of time for this holiday."

These aren't just pretty words; they're commitments. What's even more powerful is that some organizations don't limit these collective pauses to traditional holidays. They strategically choose dates in the middle of the year, often after completing a huge event or project, to ensure their teams get that crucial, collective reset.

I truly commend these organizations for walking their talk, and I've even had the privilege of incorporating this practice into my own organization. As I've said before, we cannot pour from an empty cup. It's not enough for us as leaders to understand the importance of rest; we have to walk it like we talk it and actively ensure those around us—our teams, our colleagues, our entire community—are also protecting their peace, their mental, physical, and psychological health, and their overall wealth.

If you are in a leadership position, I urge you to seriously consider incorporating these intentional, collective pause periods into your organization's rhythm. It's not just a nice perk; it's a strategic investment in your people. It can profoundly improve the climate within your organization, fostering a culture of care, reducing burnout, and ultimately leading to a more engaged, innovative, and resilient team ready to tackle any challenge. When you prioritize their well-being, you're building a stronger, healthier foundation for shared success.

Reflection Prompts for Chapter 6: The Afterglow

- What do you hope someone will describe your impact one day?

- Write a letter from your 80-year-old self to you right now.

- Describe a legacy of rest you want to pass on to the next generation.

- What are the signs you're living a life aligned with your calling?

- What would it mean for softness—not strength—to define your story?

Conclusion: Your Journey Continues

As we turn these final pages together, I want to take a real moment to just say, thank you. Thank you for stepping into this space with me, for opening your mind and heart to the incredible, life-changing power of the pause. Writing this book has been a deeply personal journey for me, a raw reflection of my path from that relentless, exhausting hustle to finding true, intentional rest. My deepest hope is that as you've read my words, you haven't just processed them intellectually, but that you've truly felt them. I hope you found those "aha!" moments, those sparks of inspiration, and those practical tools that truly empower you to cultivate more peace, more presence, and more purpose in your own beautiful life.

This isn't just a book about taking breaks, you know? It's an invitation—a heartfelt call to fundamentally shift how you see time, how you define productivity, and most importantly, how you nurture your own precious well-being. It's about taking back control, redefining what success looks like on your terms, and truly understanding that sometimes, the most profound strength lies in the softness of a well-timed, intentional pause.

Keep Pausing, Keep Growing

Here's the thing: your journey to a more intentional, rested life doesn't magically end when you close this book. In fact, darling, it's just beginning! This is an ongoing practice, a continuous, beautiful conversation with yourself and with that wise body of yours. I'm genuinely encouraging you— no, I'm urging you—to keep exploring, experimenting, and honoring your unique, sacred rhythm.

One of the most powerful ways I've found to make these lessons stick, to truly integrate them into your everyday life, is through reflection. That's exactly why I poured my heart into creating The PAUSE Reflective Journal. It's your companion, designed specifically to help you dig deeper, track your progress, and truly personalize your pause journey. It's packed with prompts and exercises that will guide you in applying every principle from this book to your unique experiences. You can find all the details on how to get your copy and start your guided reflection by visiting https://www.staciathompson.com or scanning the QR code right here.

Stay Connected

This conversation about rest, well-being, and living an intentional life is one I'm fiercely passionate about, and I want to keep it going with you! I warmly invite you to stay connected with me and with our growing community of fellow "pausers" through these various platforms:

- Tune into The PAUSE with Dr. Stacia Podcast: Come hang out with me as I dive even deeper into these themes, share fresh insights, and chat with inspiring individuals who are truly mastering the art of the pause. You can find the podcast Pause with Dr. Stacia streaming on all platforms.

- Read My Blog Posts: For ongoing reflections, practical tips, and a peek behind the curtain into my continuing pause journey, swing by my blog at https://www.staciathompson.com/#blog.

- Find Your Rhythm with My Curated Playlists: You know how powerful music can be for your soul, right? It's a fantastic tool for mindfulness and just melting away stress. I've personally curated some special playlists designed to help you unwind, find your focus, and tap into your calm. You can access them on Spotify and Apple Music.

Always remember this, my friend: your well-being isn't just important; it's your absolute greatest asset. By consciously choosing to pause, you're not just taking care of yourself; you're creating this beautiful, powerful ripple effect that touches and benefits everyone around you. So, keep listening to your body's whispers, keep embracing the strength that comes from softness, and keep living a life that is truly, deeply aligned with your most authentic values.

Thank you again for walking this path with me. May your pauses be as purposeful and profound as your actions, and may your life overflow with unwavering peace and abundant joy. This is not an end, but an invitation to begin. Your most profound legacy isn't built in the hustle, but forged when you PAUSE ON PURPOSE!

With so much gratitude,